A Different Kind of
of
Hero

Peter Leigh

Published in association with
The Basic Skills Agency

Hodder & Stoughton
A MEMBER OF THE HODDER HEADLINE GROUP

Cataloguing in Publication Data is available from the British Library.

ISBN 0 340 696974

First published 1997
Impression number   10 9 8 7 6 5 4 3 2 1
Year   2002 2001 2000 1999 1998 1997

Typeset by Fakenham Photosetting Ltd, Fakenham, Norfolk.
Printed in Great Britain for Hodder & Stoughton Educational, a division of Hodder Headline Plc, 338 Euston Road, London NW1 3BH by Athenaeum Press Ltd, Gateshead, Tyne & Wear.

A Different Kind of Hero

Contents

1	Ben Signs Up	1
2	The Row	5
3	Just a Joke	13
4	Trouble	21
5	A Hero!	26
6	Top Secret	32
7	The Visitor	36
8	The Proudest Salute	40

1

Ben Signs Up

Ben signed the paper on the desk.

'Welcome to the Air Force, Ben'
said the Captain,
and shook Ben's hand.

Ben smiled.
A great, big smile.
'Thank you, Sir,' he said.

He had done it!
He had joined the Air Force.
He had wanted to join ever since
he was a boy.
And now he had.

But Ben did not want to be a pilot.
He was too shy to be a pilot.
He did not want everyone to look at him.
He did not want everyone to point him out,
and say 'That's the pilot.'
He wanted to be one of the team,
one of the people who got the planes ready.
He wanted to be one of the team
who nobody noticed,
but who did all the work.

At the interview the Captain asked,
'Why do you want to join the Air Force, Ben?'

Ben said, 'Because I want to be one of the
team, and I want to help my country.'

The Captain smiled.

'Good,' he said.

'The Air Force needs your sort,

your kind of people.'

Ben thought to himself,

what does he mean,

'your sort' and 'your kind of people'?

The careers teacher at school

had said the same thing –

'The Air Force needs your kind.'

I'm no different to anyone else, thought Ben.

The Captain carried on.

'Yes,' he said,

'we need more young black men like yourself.

Smart, hard-working young men.'

Ben was certainly smart.

He had very short, neat hair,

a white shirt and tie,

and knife-edge trousers.

He had always been very smart.
And he had always worked very hard
both at school and at college.

'Yes, Ben,' said the Captain,
'Your mother and father will be
very proud of you.'

Ben said nothing.
His mother was dead,
and he knew that his father would not be
proud of him.
He had not told him about the Air Force.

'Goodbye Ben,' said the Captain.
'You will report for training next week.'

2

The Row

Ben walked home slowly.
He was pleased and proud,
but he was also worried.
He hadn't told his father about the Air Force
because he was waiting for the right moment,
and it never seemed to be the right moment.

Ben's father was very stern.
He was very tall with snow-white hair,
and he always wore black

because he was a minister in the local church.
He did not approve of the Air Force.

Ben said nothing when he got home,
nor for the rest of the week.
At last, on the day before
he had to report for training, he told him.

'Benjamin!' said his father.
'Benjamin, my son!'

Why can't he call me Ben like everyone else?
thought Ben.

'Benjamin! Are you crazy?'
His father looked hurt and angry.

'No!' said Ben.

'Then why are you joining this army?'

'It's not the army. It's the Air Force.'

'Don't give me clever answers.
You know what I mean.
You are black. You have no place there.'

'It's nothing to do with being black.'

'What are you saying –
it's nothing to do with being black?
It's everything to do with being black.
Do you know how black men are treated
in the army?'

'It's not like that anymore,
and it's the Air Force, not the army,
I keep telling you!
Look, I just want to be part of the team,
and help my country.'

'Your country?
This is not your country.
This has never been black people's country.
Black people are not wanted here.'

'Well, I'm wanted now.
They want me in the Air Force.'

'Yes, they want you to die for them.
And to kill for them.

8

Benjamin, Benjamin, don't you see?
This Air Force is evil.
It is about killing people.
They want you to kill people for them.
Black people.
They want you to kill your own people!'

'It's not about killing people.
It's about defending people,
and protecting people.
All people, black and white.
It's changed now, Dad.
We're all one now.
Nobody sees if you're black or white.'

'Nobody sees? Nobody sees?
What kind of fool are you, boy?
Where have you been?
It might be all right with
your friends in school.
It might be all right with
your friends in college.
But wait till you get out into the world, boy!

The real world! The white world!
Wait till you see all your nice white friends
getting all the nice jobs
and all the nice money,
and you're getting nothing!
Then you won't say nobody sees.'

'But I've got a job! In the Air Force!'

'But Benjamin, Benjamin...'

'Don't call me that,' shouted Ben.
'Call me Ben like everyone else.'

'But it is your name!
A black name!
You should be proud of it.
And you should be proud of your colour.
And you should be proud of your people.
You should not want to be one of any team.
You should want to stay with your people!'

'Just like you stayed with Mum?'

They were cruel words, but Ben was angry.

His father sagged, as if Ben had hit him.
Ben carried on.
'Going off every evening to this meeting or that
meeting! Never getting home till late!
We never saw you from one week
to the next!'

Ben's father said nothing.
Slowly he sat down,
and put his face in his hands.

Ben looked away.
After a moment he said,
'I'm sorry!'

There was a long silence.

At last his father spoke.
His voice was sad.
'Benjamin, I was the best father I could be.
But I had work to do. Important work.

And it's not easy being a black man
in a white man's world.
And it's even less easy being a minister.
I only did what I thought was for the best.'

'I know, Dad. I'm sorry!'

'And when your own son turns against you . . .'

'Oh, Dad. I haven't turned against you.
But don't you see?
This is a fresh start.
A chance to put all that black and white stuff
behind us.
And I won't be killing anybody.
I'm just looking after the planes.'

But his father just said nothing.

3

Just a Joke

The next day Ben reported to the base,
and started his training.

He loved it!

He loved the work,
and he loved the life.
And he was very good.
He was the best on the base.
His job was to make sure that

when a plane landed,
the engine was properly shut down.
Then he had to check the engine
so that it was OK for take-off.

The work was difficult and dangerous,
because the jet engines were so hot,
and because they had to be ready again
so quickly.
The other men knew the work
was difficult and dangerous,
and they knew Ben was very good at it.

After six months' training
Ben was top of his class.
But he wasn't just best at his job,
he also had the smartest uniform,
the sharpest creases,
and the shiniest boots.

He loved the Air Force,
and he loved the work,
but most of all Ben loved

being one of the team.

There were six of them –
Ben and Dave worked on the engine,
Andy and Rob checked the cockpit and
the controls, and
Mick and Pete refilled the fuel tank.
They could get a plane ready
faster than any other team.

When Ben worked with them,
he felt a warm glow inside.
They were the best!

One day Dave got black oil
smeared across his face.
'Look at me,' he said, 'I'm Ben,'
and the others laughed.
'At least you can wash it off,' said Rob,
and they laughed some more.

Ben smiled,
but he didn't say anything.

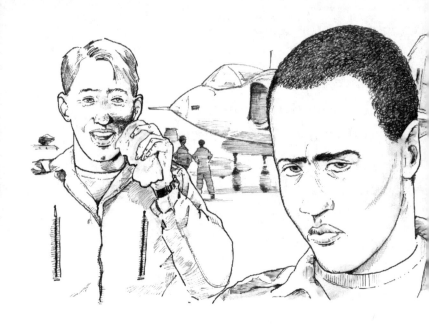

He didn't know what to say.
He felt confused.
What did they mean?

The next day they got a plane ready.
It was flying to Africa.
'It's going to bongo-bongo land,' said Dave.
'I bet Ben wishes he was on it.'

'What do you mean?' said Ben.
He sounded angry.

It seemed so stupid!

'It's a joke, Ben. Just a joke,' said Dave.
'Can't you take a joke?'

Ben turned away,
and the men laughed.

And then Ben began to hear other things,
things that were whispered behind his back,
or when they thought he couldn't hear.

At first he tried to ignore them.
He thought that was the best thing to do.
He thought that if he pretended
he hadn't heard and said nothing,
then they would get fed up and stop.

But they didn't get fed up,
and they didn't stop.
Ben began to hear jokes everywhere,
even where they weren't meant.

If someone laughed,
Ben thought it was a joke about him.
If someone said the word 'black',
Ben thought he was talking about him.

He started to complain.

'What are you talking about, Ben?'
said the others.
'It's just a joke.
You must learn to take it.'

He tried to make jokes himself.
But they didn't work.
Nobody laughed.

And the work suffered.
The team started to fall apart.
They blamed Ben.

One day a very large plane landed at the base.
It needed a special ladder
to reach the engines.

'Ben doesn't need that,' said Dave.
'He doesn't need a ladder.
He can climb anything without a ladder.'

'What do you mean by that?' said Ben angrily.

'You know,' said Dave.
'Back in the jungle.
Up in the tree-tops.'

'What? . . .' said Ben,
and turned on Dave.
'Take it easy, Ben,' said the others.
'It's a joke! Just a joke!'

Ben stared angrily for a moment or two,
and then turned away.
As he did so Dave made a noise
like a monkey.
'Hoo-hoo-hoo-hoo!'

That was too much for Ben.
On top of everything else it was too much.

He exploded.

He grabbed the first thing that came to hand –
it was a big spanner –
and charged at Dave.
'I'll get you, you b......!' he yelled.

The others got between them,
and held Ben off,
but he was still fighting and yelling
and kicking.

'STOP THAT NOW!'
It was the Captain.
'ALL OF YOU!
STAND TO ATTENTION!'

The men's training was good.
Their arms dropped to their sides,
and they all stood still.
Ben was panting.

'IN MY OFFICE NOW!'

4

Trouble

The men were all lined up against the wall
in the Captain's office.
They were all at attention.
Their arms were pressed to their sides,
and their eyes were straight to the front.
They had told the Captain
what had happened,
and had said they were sorry.

'You fools,' said the Captain.

'You stupid fools!
All that work, all that training,
and you want to waste it.
You want to throw it all away.
And why?
For some stupid little joke.
I hope you're proud of yourselves.
Now listen to me, and listen good.
You were the best team on the base.
You were the fastest,
and just because of that
I am going to say no more about this.
But get yourselves together!
Get back to being the best!
And if anything like this ever happens again,
then you will all be out!
OUT!
Do you understand me?
I said DO YOU UNDERSTAND ME?'

'Yes Sir!' they all said together.

'Now get out!' said the Captain,

and all the men turned and marched out.

'Not you Ben!' he said at the last minute,
and Ben halted, and turned round.
The Captain waited until the sound of
marching died away.

'Now listen, Ben,' he said.
'I'm disappointed in you.
You were the best man in this team,
but now you're ruining it.
You're ruining it
because of your silly moaning.
This is the Air Force.
We are men in the Air Force!
Not a bunch of school kids!
We can't start to cry every time
someone says something nasty to us.'

'But sir,' blurted out Ben.
'It wasn't my fault. That was racism.
You can't let them get away with . . .'

'Be quiet!' shouted the Captain.
'Don't tell me what it was or wasn't,
and don't tell me what I can or can't do!
Now, you were the best man,
and you can be the best man again.
I want you to be the best man again,
but you will have to pull yourself together.
Remember, Ben, you are part of the team.
Now you will forget all about
what happened today, and
if anyone says anything like it to you again,

you will ignore it. Is that clear?'

Ben was silent.

'I said is that clear?'

'Yes sir!'

'Good, and don't forget it!
Now go!'

Ben turned, and marched out.

The Captain watched him go.
The trouble is, he thought to himself,
they're all the same.

5

A Hero!

Ben went back to work.
The team went back to work.
Everything seemed to be the same.
But it wasn't.
Everything was different.
Nobody spoke.
The work was done in silence.

Nobody made any more jokes about Ben,
but nobody made any more jokes at all.

Ben did the same job as before,
but inside he felt sick.
He didn't feel part of the team anymore.
He felt as if they blamed him
for what had happened.

At night he lay awake in his bunk.
All the things he had loved,
all his dreams about life in the Air Force,
had turned to ashes.

One day there was a special practice.
The pilot of the plane was going to
pretend to be hurt, so that the team had
to deal with him as well as the plane.
The team had practised this many times,
and were very good at it.

It all depended on Ben.
He had to shut down the engine first,
before the others could deal with the pilot,
and check the plane,
and refill it with fuel.

This was difficult and dangerous.
But Ben knew he could do it.

They had to wait for the signal.
When it came they raced for the plane.
Ben stood underneath it.
He could feel the tremendous heat
from the jet engine just above his head.
The others were looking at him,
waiting for him to shut the engine down.
Ben reached up to start.
And then Dave stepped on a patch of oil,
and slipped.
Without thinking he grabbed a fuel line to save
himself. He pulled the line off,
and fuel sprayed everywhere.

Ben heard a scream behind him.
He saw the fuel spilling on the ground
and spraying in the air.
If it touched the engine,
it would blow up, together with the team,
the plane, and half the base.

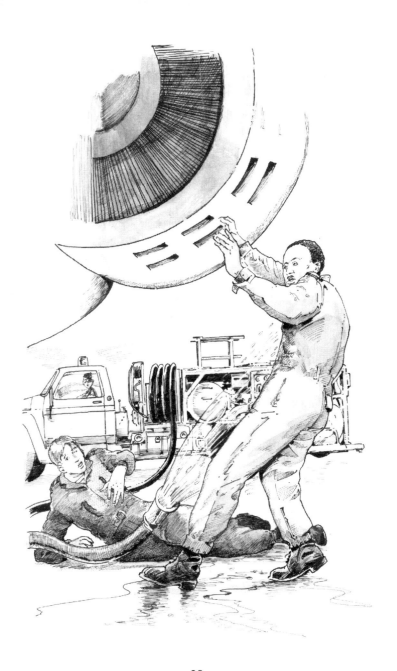

Ben felt his insides turn to water.
And then his training took over.
He turned back to the engine,
and carried on.
He worked very quickly but very carefully.
He tried to shield the engine
from the spraying fuel
with his body.
He tried not to think about what would
happen if the fuel caught alight.

He did it!
He shut down the engine.
It was safe!

Ben had saved himself,
the team, the pilot, and the plane.

They all crowded round him.
They shook his hand,
and clapped him on his back.
'You saved our lives, Ben,' they said.

They took him to the canteen,
and bought him drinks.
They cheered him,
and told him how good he was.

He was a hero!

But Ben didn't feel a hero.
Inside it didn't mean anything.
Inside he still felt sick.

6

Top Secret

Ben was in the papers and on television.
The Captain made sure of that.
The Air Force needed a hero,
and a black hero was even better.
He called Ben to his office.

'We are proud of you, Ben,' he said.
'The Air Force is proud of you.
Your people are proud of you.'

Ben stood to attention.
His eyes looked straight ahead.
My people? he thought.
Who are they? But he said nothing.

The Captain carried on.
'You are going to get a medal, Ben.
You are the first man
to get this medal for years.
There's going to be a special parade
on Saturday,
and you will be presented with it.
The television and the papers will be there,
and it will be presented to you
by a Very Important Person.
This is top secret of course,
but it's....'
The Captain whispered a name in Ben's ear.
'Now what do you think of that?'

Ben said nothing.

'She's had to cancel other things,

but after what you did
she wanted to present you with the medal
herself.'

Ben still said nothing.

'So you better get your best uniform ready,
and start polishing your boots for Saturday.'

'Yes sir.'

'Aren't you pleased?'

'Yes sir.'

'Or excited?'

'Yes sir.'

'You don't seem to be.'

'Oh, I am sir.
Very pleased. And very excited.

Can I go now sir?'

'Yes, of course.'

Ben saluted smartly, turned, and marched out.

Strange, thought the Captain,
he doesn't seem to care.
Mind you, you can never tell with his kind.

7

The Visitor

Saturday was bright and clear.
The whole base had been cleaned.
The fences had been painted,
and the grass had been cut.

Lots of visitors came.
There were officers with swords and
white gloves, and ladies in big hats.

Ben looked superb.

His boots shone,
and you could cut yourself on his creases.
His badges glinted in the sunlight.

The men were just about to go on parade,
when Ben had a message
from the guards at the gate –

'We're holding a man here.
He says he's your father.'
Ben's heart started pounding.
What was his father doing here?

Ben hurried down to the guardhouse.
His father was standing by himself
in the corner.
He was standing very still and upright,
and his white hair shone.

'Dad, what are you doing here?'

'Benjamin, my son.
That was a brave thing you did.

I read about it in the paper,
and my heart filled with pride.
Benjamin, why did you not tell me?'

Ben looked at his father.
He had wanted to tell him all about it.
About the medal,
and about the fight,
and about the insults,
and about laying awake at night feeling sick.
He had wanted to tell him,
but he hadn't.

'I'm sorry,' he started,
and then suddenly broke off.
He looked up.

'Come with me, Dad,' he said.

He took his father to the square.
There was a part roped off for visitors.
It was already full of officers and ladies.

They looked surprised when Ben
led his father up.

'Wait here, Dad,' said Ben.
He told him what was going to happen
in the parade.
'I'll come and get you as soon as it's over,'
he said, and then he rushed back
to join the others.

8

The Proudest
Salute

'Parade.....Atten......SHUN!'

Five hundred men crashed to attention.
They were all lined up behind Ben
who was standing by himself
in the middle of the square.

A helicopter appeared in the sky.
It dropped down,

and landed at the edge of the square.

A red carpet was quickly unrolled.
The door opened,
and the Very Important Person stepped out.
The cameras flashed,
everybody cheered,
and the band played 'God Save the Queen.'

The Captain saluted with his sword,
and his wife curtsied.

The Very Important Person
walked down the red carpet
with the Captain at her side.
At the end was a small platform
with a microphone by it.
The Very Important Person stood
on the platform,
and the Captain read a speech.
It told everyone what Ben had done.

Ben didn't listen to a word of it.

While the Captain's voice was booming round
the square, Ben's eyes were searching the
visitors' part. Where was his father?
Where was he?

And then he saw him.

He was standing right at the very end
by himself. Alone.
None of the officers or the ladies
were standing near him.

He was standing very still,
like a statue carved from stone.
As Ben looked, the wind blew across
the square and lifted his hair a little.

The Captain finished speaking.
He signalled to Ben.
Ben marched forward.
The Very Important Person smiled at him,
and reached forward to pin the medal
on his uniform. Everyone clapped.

She straightened up, and Ben stepped back.
The applause died away.
Everyone looked at Ben.
He was meant to march back to his place.
But he didn't.

He stood to attention, and waited.

And waited.

He waited until the whole square was silent,
and all eyes were on him.

And then he turned,
and marched past the Very Important Person,
past the Captain,
past the officers with their swords,
past the ladies with their big hats,
to the figure at the end.

He halted in front of his father,
and they looked at each other.

For a long time.

And then Ben brought his arm up slowly
in a salute.
It was the longest and proudest salute
of his life.

And then he turned and marched back
to his place.